VAGN HOLMBOE

THE WEE WEE MAN

for mixed voices

Op. 110 b

WILHELM HANSEN, MUSIK-FORLAG, COPENHAGEN

The wee wee man

As I was walking all alone,
between a water and a wa',
And there I spy'd a wee wee man,
And he was the least that ere I saw.

His legs were scarce a shathmont's lenght,
And thick and thimber was his thighs,
Between his brows there was a span,
And between his shoulders there was three.

He took up a meikle stane
And he flang't as far as I could see
Though I had been a Wallace wight
I coudna liften't to my knee.

O wee wee man, but thou be strong
O tell me where thy dwelling be?
My dwelling's down at yon' bonny bower
And will you go with me and see?

On we lap and awa we rade
Till we came to yon bonny green
We 'lighted down for to bait our horse
And out there came a lady fine.

Four-and-twenty at her back
And they were a'clad out in green
Though the king of Scotland had been there
The warst o'them might ha' been his queen.

On we lap and awa we rade
Till we came to yon bonny ha'
Where the roof was o'the beaten gould
And the floor was o' the crystal a'

When we came to the stair foot
Ladies were dancing jimp and sma'
But in the twinkling of an eye
My wee wee man was clean awa.

the
wee
wee
man

A Border Ballad
for
mixed voices

Note! The composer alters the distribution of voices within the work

Edition Wilhelm Hansen A/S, Copenhagen

THE WEE WEE MAN

Vagn Holmboe

6

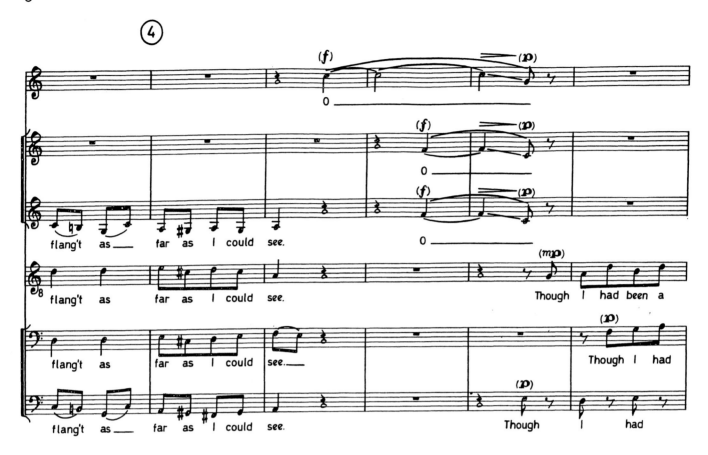

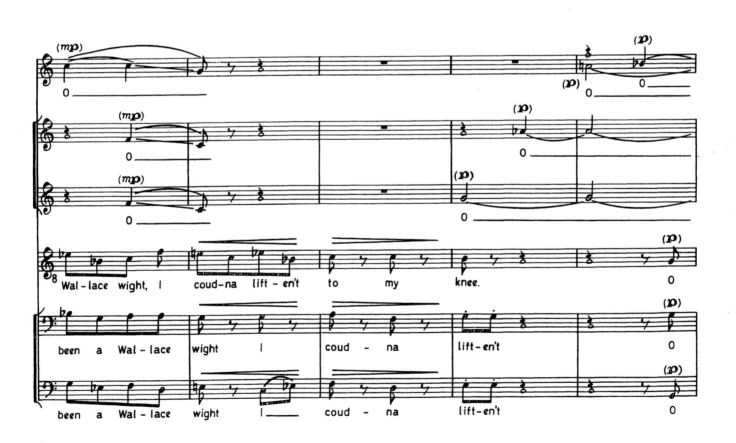

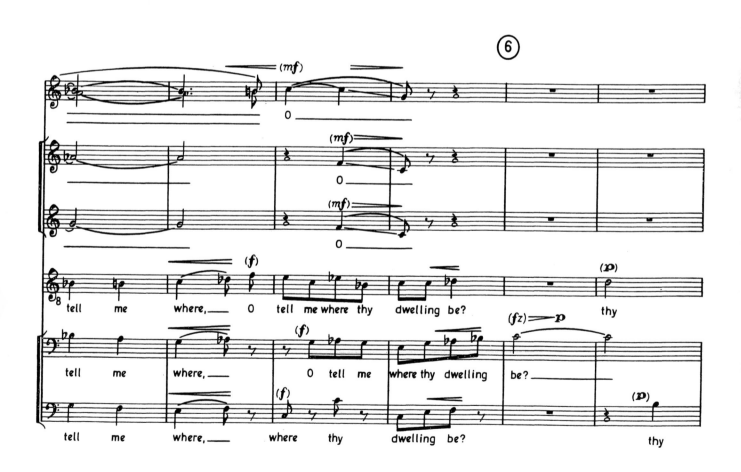

29.153

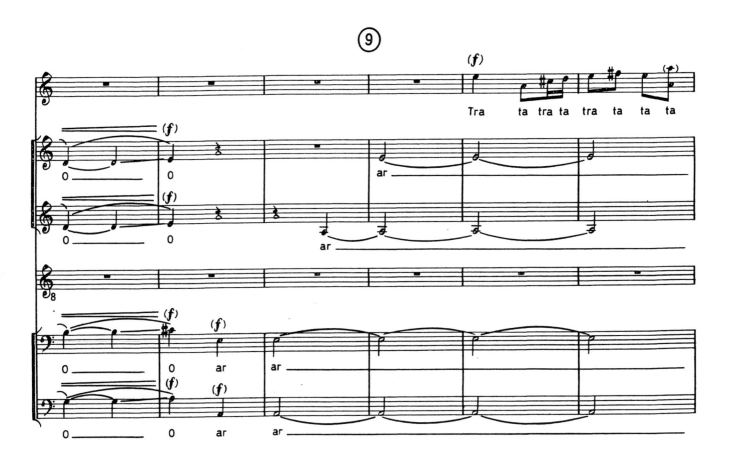

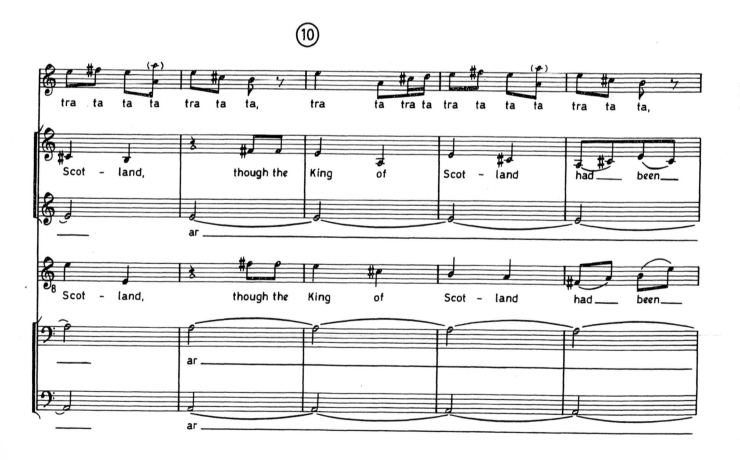

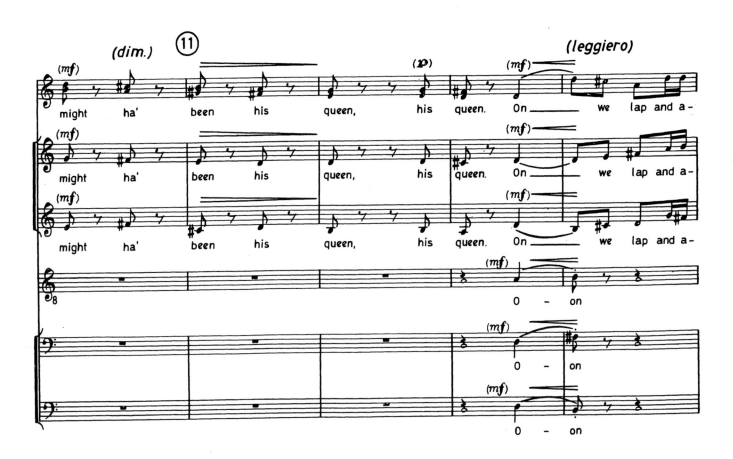

(tenuto)

14

(leggiero)

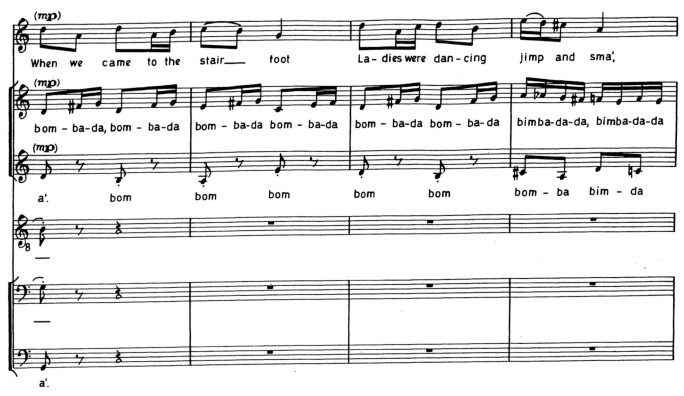

⑬